# GIFTS
# FOR
# YOUR CAT

**GIFTS FOR YOUR CAT**
**A READER'S DIGEST BOOK**

Produced by Tucker Slingsby Ltd.

**Copyright © 1995 Tucker Slingsby Ltd.**

Library of Congress Cataloging in Publication Data

Gifts for your cat.
      p.   cm.
"A Reader's digest book"—T.p.  verso.
ISBN  0-89577-792-4
1.  Cats—Equipment and supplies.
2.  Handicraft.  3.  Gifts.
I.  Reader's Digest Association.
SF447.3.G54   1995
636.8'0028—dc20                   95-9067

Illustrations by Roger Fereday
Step-by-step diagrams by John Hutchinson
Special thanks to Blair Brown Hoyt, Bob Mathias,
Cheryl Owen, and Sandy Ransford

Printed in Singapore

# GIFTS
# FOR
# YOUR CAT

Reader's
Digest

The Reader's Digest Association, Inc.
Pleasantville, N.Y. / Montreal

# Contents

## FOR GOURMET CATS

## PURR-FECT PRESENTATION

# For Playful Cats

Little kittens, or grown-up cats for that matter, will treat most of your household possessions as toys, if you let them. The trick is to provide a few lovingly crafted inventions to divert the relentless curiosity in your cat.

# Fast Fun

Cats are like kids. Drop a fortune on the hottest new-fangled toy and they're sure to reject it for your one-hundred-per-cent recycled oldies but goldies. Designed to be made in thirty seconds or less, these interactive gizmos are sure to give you and your playmate hours of mindless fun. The couch potato can tie a toy on to a stick and wave it from the comfort of an armchair.

## Shoelace Snake

Encourage your little Leo's jungle instinct to chase and pounce with this instant toy. Tie two old shoelaces together, then tie knots at 4-in. intervals along their combined length. Wiggle this shoelace snake along the floor and watch your cat become a hunter.

## Box of Tricks

You'll need a large cardboard box with plenty of room for cat cavorting. Round up the most cat-friendly trinkets you can scavenge and deposit your appealing collection in the box. Some winning choices are crunchy, dried leaves, mouse-

sized corks or crumpled-up balls of newspaper or cellophane. Frequently changing your selection of toys will ensure ongoing revelry in your new rec room.

## Rustling Up Some Fun

Cats love frolicking with dried flowers and grasses, especially if they're part of your favorite flower arrangement. Strips of thin poster board make a more durable substitute. Cut the strips about 18 in. long and ½ in. wide and tie them in a bunch. Brandish your bouquet or rustle it along the floor.

## Dangling Corks

Take six corks and knot about 12 in. of string around each. Tie them in a row to the arm of a chair or on a coathanger that can be hung securely. Get the fat off your cat by putting the toy just out of reach. You've never seen such aerobics!

## Great Balls of Fun

Watch your cat go wild playing soccer with a small, plastic ball. For an extra-special gift, decorate a regular ping-pong ball with your cat's name and a painted paw-print. Or decorate the ball's two halves in contrasting colors. This will make it especially eye-catching as it bounces its way about your home.

# Climbing Tree

Climbing and clawing are what your cat enjoys most. And, if nothing else is on offer, your energetic pet may turn into a monster attacking your soft

## Materials Needed

- Pine: 36 in. x 3 in. x 3 in. (for post)
- Pine: 16 in. x 1 in. x 1 in. (for supporting the post)
- Plywood: 24 in. x 24 in. x ¾ in. (for base)
- Wooden dowel: 32 in. x 1 in.
- Non-toxic wood glue
- Screws: 2 x no. 12, 3 in. long
- Rope: 60 ft. x ½ in. diameter
- Flat-headed nails: 4
- Hand brace with wood drill bits
- Hammer, screwdriver, saw, and sandpaper

furnishings. So, if your cat can't get to the great outdoors, this climbing tree will make the perfect present.

The simple frame costs only a few dollars and is easy to make. It doubles as a scratching post, climbing jungle gym, even a play area. The tree has been very carefully designed to hold even the plumpest cat without toppling. So builders beware – don't be tempted to tamper with the dimensions.

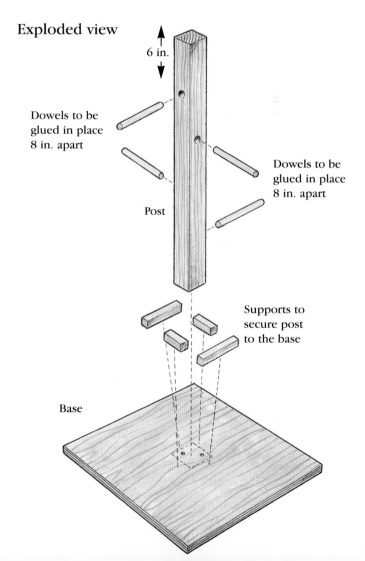

Exploded view

6 in.

Dowels to be glued in place 8 in. apart

Dowels to be glued in place 8 in. apart

Post

Supports to secure post to the base

Base

**1** Cut post and base to correct size. Using a hand brace, drill four 1 in. holes in the post for climbing dowels. The holes must be at least 1½ in. deep. Position the top one 6 in. down, then space them 8 in. apart.

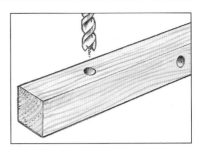

**2** Drill two pilot holes through the center of the base for the screws. These will secure the base to the post. Glue and screw base to post. Use glue generously, following the manufacturer's instructions.

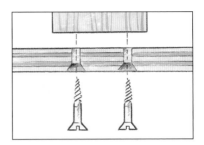

**3** Cut four 8 in. climbing dowels and glue each one securely into the post. For added strength at the base, glue short pieces of wood around the join of the post and base. Apply plenty of adhesive to ensure a really firm join.

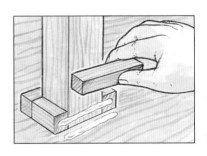

**4** Wrap the length of rope around the post. Start at the base and go up to just below the top dowel. Secure the rope at both ends with two flat-headed nails. Lightly sand all the exposed wood to smooth and prevent splinters.

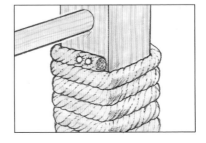

# Marvelous Mouse

What self-respecting cat can turn up its nose at a mouse? This quick-to-make soft toy will be the centerpiece of your cat's toy collection – it's likely to be so popular that you will need to make a new one every few months. Use fake fur for a fluffy effect or neon-colored cotton or wool to make a truly jazzy mouse toy.

Fill the mouse with scraps of fabric, pantyhose, or polyester fiberfill and don't forget to include the Secret Ingredient, dried catnip.

The mouse tail can be a shoelace or a piece of ribbon or string, knotted at the end to prevent fraying. Paint on the eyes and nose or make them from felt, securely sewn on. Your cat will chase this alluring creature for hours.

## Materials Needed

- Fabric for body: 12 in. square
- Felt for ears: 3 in. square
- Scraps of felt for eyes and nose (optional)
- Fabric pen
- Polyester fiberfill
- Leather shoelace, ribbon, or string about 10 in. long
- Dried catnip
- Glue
- Pencil and paper
- Basic sewing equipment

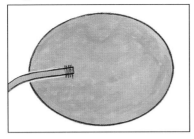

**1** Trace patterns for body and ear from the template opposite. Cut three body pieces from felt or fabric. On the wrong side of one piece, machine stitch the tail cord firmly in place in the position marked.

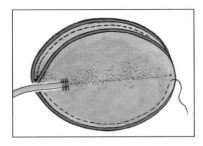

**2** With right sides together, machine stitch two pieces together along one edge, using a ¼ in. seam allowance. Stitch the third shape to the first, leaving a small gap between the two seams for the tail to poke through.

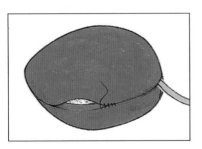

**3** Stitch the remaining edge of the third piece to the second piece, leaving a 1 in. gap in the seam for turning. Turn right side out and pull the tail through. Stuff the mouse firmly, then slipstitch the opening closed.

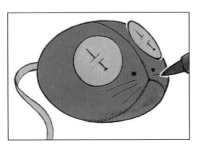

**4** Cut two ear pieces from felt or fabric. Pin the ears on the mouse to check position, then glue in place. Draw on eyes, nose, and whiskers with a fabric pen, sew on scraps of felt, or use embroidery.

Don't make your mouse smaller than this template or your cat may be tempted to swallow it.

EAR
cut 2

BODY
cut 3

Attach tail
here

# Flying Fishes

Kitten cats will leap to the heavens for this down-to-earth mobile, trying to catch the windblown flying fishes. Position it in a breezy position, and the fish will wriggle. When the elements of your mobile are assembled, hang it up and carefully slide the threads until it balances. Then glue the threads to the dowels. Hang the mobile just out of reach, so that kitty has to stretch and jump to reach it.

## Materials Needed

- Colored poster board
- Wooden dowel:
    two pieces, 8 in. x ⅜ in.
    one piece, 12 in. x ⅜ in.
- Heavy thread or string
- Black felt-tip pen
- Hole-punch
- Scissors
- Hacksaw
- Cloth ribbon: 60 in.
- Non-toxic wood glue
- Pencil and paper

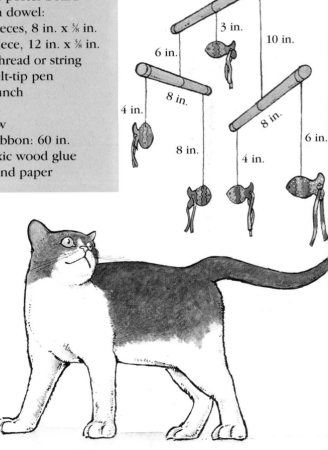

**1** Trace the fish template on page 59 onto poster board. Cut out five fish. With the felt-tip pen, draw in the eyes and scales. Punch a hole in the center of each tail and tie a 12 in. length of ribbon through the hole.

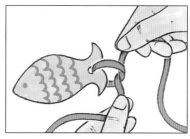

**2** Cut five 20 in. lengths of heavy thread. Fold each in half. Make a hole at the top of each fish. Insert the ends of one length of thread through the hole in each fish. Pass the ends back through the loop and tighten as shown.

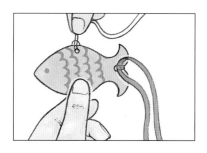

**3** Tie a fish on each end of an 8 in. dowel. Adjust the lengths of the threads according to the diagram. Repeat with the second pair. (Note that the lengths can be different). Tie the last fish to the center of the long dowel.

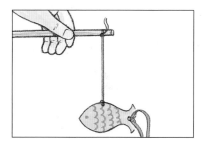

**4** Cut three 24 in. lengths of thread and fold in half. Loop one around the center of each short dowel then tie to the end of the long dowel. Tie the last thread to the center of the long dowel. Adjust lengths for balance, then glue in place.

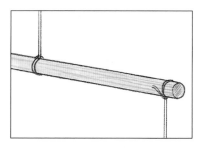

# For Comfort-loving Cats

A cat is the ultimate domestic heat-seeking missile! Find the warmest spot in the house and you'll find kitty, snoozing the day away. To make for one happy cat, set up the corner to be comfortable as well as cozy.

# Kitty Pillow

Whiling the hours away, curled up in a ball, cats enjoy recharging in their own little world. Part of their slumbering nook must be a comfy pillow. A special cover for such a pillow is simple to sew and you can make it to fit your cat's basket or favorite chair. So that everyone knows who owns this pillow, appliqué a motif that suits your cat's personality. You can choose from the selections on pages 60 and 61.

## Materials Needed

- Square or rectangular purchased pillow form
- Cotton fabric for cover
- Cotton fabric for motif: 12 in. square
- Double-sided fusable interfacing: 12 in. square
- Embroidery thread or bits of felt to contrast with cat motif
- Paper and pencil
- Basic sewing equipment

**1** Cut out two squares or rectangles of fabric exactly the same size as the purchased pillow form. Do not be tempted to make the cover bigger than the pillow or it will be too flat.

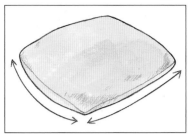

**2** To make the appliqué motif, iron interfacing onto the wrong side of the contrasting fabric. Trace a motif (see pages 60–61) onto paper, enlarging as desired. Pin the pattern onto interfaced fabric and cut out the motif.

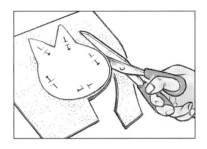

**3** Pin the motif, right side up, onto the right side of the pillow top. Fuse in position with an iron. Sew around the edge by hand or machine. Stitch features using stem stitch (see page 64) and embroidery thread. Sew felt eyes and nose in place.

**4** Pin the top and bottom pieces, wrong sides together. Sew around edges, leaving an opening on one side for turning. Turn right side out and insert the pillow form. Hand or machine stitch closed.

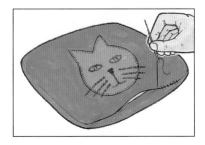

# Lap Mat

The number one destination for a resting cat is your lap. But this can result in a legload of cat hairs and snagged panty hose. This padded lap mat provides the perfect answer. Draped over your knees, it will guard your clothes and keep your cat snug. It can also be used to cover chair seats.

This washable mat is made from velour on top to make your cat feel pampered and cotton on the bottom. The batting in the middle offers additional comfort for the cat and much-needed protection for your clothes.

## Materials Needed
- Washable velour:
  36 in. x 24 in.
- Cotton fabric:
  36 in. x 24 in.
- Medium weight batting:
  36 in. x 24 in.
- Embroidery thread in contrasting color (optional)
- Basic sewing equipment

**1** Place the two pieces of fabric right sides together. Put the piece of batting on top. Pin the three layers together, then baste.

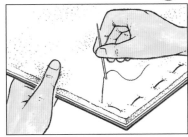

**2** Machine stitch around all sides, leaving a 6 in. opening in one side. Trim edges and corners.

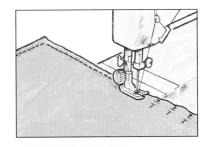

**3** Turn the mat right side out. Hand or machine stitch the opening closed.

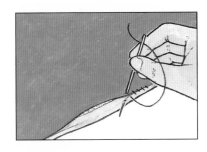

**4** Topstitch by machine along all edges, about 1 in. in from edge. Or, embroider a decorative stitch in contrasting thread.

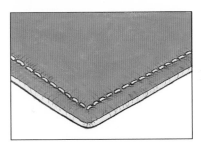

# Cat-nap Sack

There is nothing a cat loves more than a private place to snuggle down for an afternoon snooze. This kitty sleeping bag offers warmth and a retreat from the stresses and strains of being an idle feline. It can be placed in your cat's basket or any favorite sleeping nook.

Designed to allow your cat to burrow inside easily, the cat-nap sack is simple to make even for those without much sewing know-how.

Choose the color carefully. The sack will look best if it complements the color of your cat or of your decor. For added kitty enjoyment, include some of your pet's beloved toys.

## Materials Needed

- Quilted fabric: 90 in. x at least 36 in. wide
- Bias binding: 144 in. x 1 in. wide
- Teacup
- Pencil and paper
- Ruler
- Basic sewing equipment

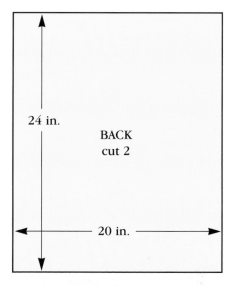

24 in.

**BACK
cut 2**

20 in.

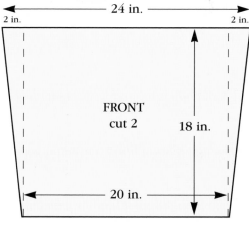

24 in.

2 in.                                    2 in.

**FRONT
cut 2**

18 in.

20 in.

**1** Make a pattern for the front and back, as shown on previous page. From quilted fabric, cut two fronts and two backs. Pin the two front pieces together with wrong sides together, then baste.

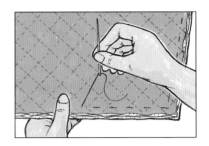

**2** Open out one edge of the bias binding so you can see the fold line. Baste to the longest edge of the bag front, so that the fold line is positioned ⅜ in. from the fabric edge. Machine stitch in place.

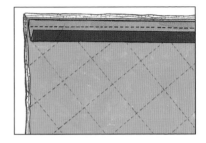

**3** Fold binding over to back of fabric so that it extends ⅛ in. beyond the previous stitching line. Baste. From the front, machine stitch the edge through all thicknesses.

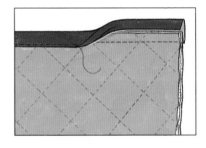

**4** Place the two back pieces wrong sides together. Baste around all edges. Pin the front section in place and baste along the sides and bottom through all thicknesses.

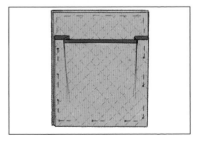

**5** To make curved corners, place a teacup on the corner of the bag and draw a pencil line around it; cut along the curved line. Repeat on the remaining three corners.

**6** Trim the outer edges with bias binding (see steps 2 and 3). Turn under the raw end of the binding and overlap at the finishing point.

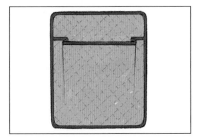

# For Cats About Town

The sophisti-cat will take pride in displaying *haute couture* accessories. With a range of eye-catching baubles to highlight everything from elegant dinner wear to more sporty apparel, the neighborhood's premier fashion plate will feel at ease entertaining friends on any occasion.

# Nifty Neckwear

Alley cats who patrol the neighborhood do just fine with an ordinary collar and ID. But to make your kitty feel truly spoiled, you can create a special party collar for indoors.

A decorated store-bought collar will enliven surprise parties, but a custom-designed collar made to measure will best reflect your kitty's personality. Design a collar to suit your cat – proud, playful, or cute – or all of the above.

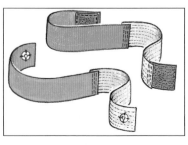

When making a cat's indoor collar, always sew in a 1½ in. elastic section, so that your cat can safely pull its head out of the collar if necessary. For simplicity, fasten the collar with a press stud or use Velcro.

## Paints and inks

If you're running out of time, decorate a store-bought collar. The simplest way is to paint a pattern on a colorful collar with indelible marker pens or fabric paints.

## Elegant evenings

For tigers of the night, make an evening collar from generous lengths of gold and silver ribbon. Braid together five strands of narrow ribbon. Add the elastic section and a gold buckle to complete the cosmopolitan effect.

## Velvet nights

Sleek, blonde cats adore rich velvet ribbon in black, navy, or burgundy. Add a dark-colored elastic segment and fasten with Velcro.

## Lacy luxury

Gathered lace can make a feminine feline feel frisky, but don't let the romantic appeal of the collar distract you from the important elastic section.

## Sparkling strands

For the Hollywood wannabe, sew together glittering silk and shimmering metallic ribbons. This collar is a real eye-dazzler!

## Priceless pearls

Midnight-hued cats look splendid in pearls. More subtle than diamonds, pearls can be added to any fabric collar, simply by using pearlized puffy fabric paint.

## Bow ties

Tasteful toms wouldn't dream of party-going without a carefully chosen bow tie. Made from dark silk, satin, or velvet ribbon, a well-tied bow can create a truly masculine effect. First make a basic ribbon collar, then tie on the bow. The elastic section will be concealed beneath the bow.

## Fancy free

Embroidered braid collars offer a certain *je ne sais quoi*. A wide braid can be used on its own with just the elastic section and Velcro added. Or you can glue the braid to the non-elastic part of a store-bought collar.

## Checked out

A strip of gingham fabric with a narrow piece of grosgrain ribbon sewn along the center to stiffen it looks cool at summer parties. Fasten with elastic and Velcro.

# Kitty Kit-bag

What better accessory for the globe-trotting cat than a colorful tote bag to transport personal grooming necessities.

If your cat makes regular appearances at cat shows and other celebrity occasions, the need for a stylish carry-all is obvious. Brown-paper bags simply don't cut it.

Even homebodies appreciate a kit-bag that keeps their brushes and combs together.

And for you it's a great way of ensuring that cat hairs end up in the bag and not on your furniture.

To make the bag more distinctive, you can decorate it with fabric-painted paw prints. If time is short, you can paint these freehand, but for a more polished result follow the step-by-step instructions for stenciling shown on the opposite page.

## Materials Needed

- Cotton fabric:
    12 in. x 36 in.
- Thick cord: 54 in.
- Basic sewing equipment

## Decoration

- Fabric paints in 3 colors
- Stencil board or acetate:
    approx. 6 in. square
- Craft knife
- Cutting mat
- Masking tape
- Flat paintbrush
- Ceramic tile or old plate
- Stencil brush
- Safety pin

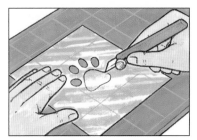

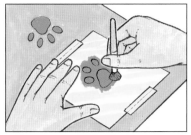

**1** To stencil paw prints, use the template on page 59. Trace the shape onto stencil board or acetate. Working on a cutting mat, use a craft knife to cut the stencil. Position the stencil on the fabric and hold with masking tape. Be sure to place the stencil at least 2 in. inside the edge of the fabric.

**2** Apply a thin film of fabric paint to the tile with the flat brush. Holding the stencil brush upright, dab into the paint and then through the stencil. Allow to dry, then move the stencil to another part of the fabric. Clean the stencil before changing colors. Decorate one side of the fabric.

**3** Press the fabric, following directions given by the paint manufacturer. Fold fabric in half, right sides together, so that paw prints are on one side. Pin, then stitch along each side, using a ½ in. seam allowance. Press seams open.

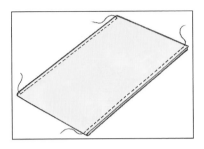

**4** Leave bag inside out and mark ¼ in. from the top. Turn and press. Mark 1½ in. from folded edge. Turn, press, and baste near top edge. Machine stitch through both layers ⅛ in. from lower edge, leaving ½ in. gap to insert cord.

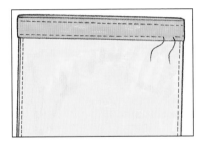

**5** To strengthen the channel, machine stitch again around top edge of bag.

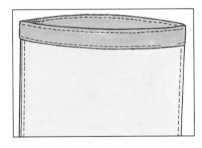

**6** Attach a safety pin or bodkin to one end of the cord. Thread through opening in cord channel. Remove safety pin and knot ends. Turn the bag right side out.

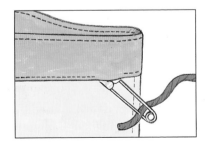

# Kitten Mitten

After a thorough brushing to remove loose hairs and tangles, there's nothing a stylish cat enjoys more than to be stroked by silk or velvet. Use this special mitten to make your cat's coat glisten.

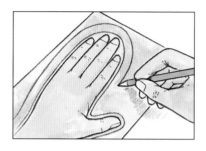

## Materials Needed

- Velvet or silk:
  12 in. x 24 in.
- Paper: a little larger than your hand
- Pencil
- Matching thread
- Contrasting thread

**1** Place your hand on the paper and draw around it. Outline thumb separately. Now draw a second outline 1 in. outside the first. Cut around the outside line.

**2** Fold fabric in half lengthwise, right sides together. Pin mitten pattern to fabric and draw around it. Cut out shape.

**3** Pin mitten pieces right sides together. Machine stitch around edges, using ¼ in. seam allowance. Clip seams. Measure ¼ in. from wrist edge. Turn and press. Repeat. Machine stitch through all layers to hem. Turn mitten right side out.

# Framed Felines

A sensitive cat might feel slighted if excluded from your collection of family photos on the mantel. The picture should accentuate your cat's best features and be prominently positioned in your gallery alongside your other family portraits.

## Materials Needed

- Purchased wooden frame
- Plain paper or gift wrap
- Tracing paper
- Pencil
- Scissors
- Glue
- Clear varnish and brush
- Fine-grade sandpaper

Be a surreptitious shutter-bug – shield your camera until the last possible moment. Try creeping up while your kitty is getting some shut-eye. Whisper, "Tuna fish." Then as the expectation of dinner wafts into your feline's consciousness and registers in the opening of an eye, snap that perfect picture. For action shots, you'll need a partner to provide fun and games off camera.

Once you have a dashing, demure, or decorative picture of puss, you'll want to show-case it in a fancy frame. Choose a plain frame and decorate it with fish, mice, or paw prints to give that personal touch.

36

**1** Cut out motifs from gift wrap or trace the motifs of your choice from pages 58–63. Cut a template for each one, reducing or enlarging as required.

**2** Using the templates as a guide, cut out the shapes in different colors of paper. Make as many shapes as you need to decorate the frame. Add eyes, noses, whiskers, and scales as needed.

**3** Arrange the shapes around the frame, then glue in place. Allow to dry.

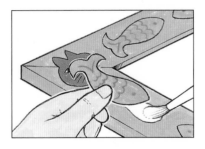

**4** Apply a coat of varnish to the decorated frame. Allow it to dry completely, then sand lightly. Apply a second coat of varnish. Make sure the varnish is dry before inserting your feline's photo.

# Feline File

Whether your kitty is an aristocat or one of dubious ancestry, a filing system for essential paperwork is a must.

A feline file is the ideal solution for organizing and storing pedigree documents, veterinary records, and show rosettes as well as family photographs.

Personalize a ring binder by covering it with decorated paper. If your cat has an active social life, add a daily planner to the front of the binder to keep track of all those party invitations and appointments at the beauty parlor.

## Materials Needed

- Purchased ring binder
- Colored paper
- Clear plastic pockets
- Self-adhesive, clear plastic film
- Sheets of thin poster board
- Adhesive photo corners

## Decorations

- Paint
- Stencil board or acetate
- Craft knife
- Cutting mat
- Masking tape
- Ceramic tile or old plate
- Stencil brush

**1** To decorate your own paper, stencil paw prints or other motifs onto plain-colored paper. For motifs see pages 58-63. For stenciling instructions see page 33.

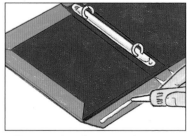

**2** Cut the decorated paper 1 in. larger than the binder on all sides. Center the binder on the paper. Trim corners. Turn edges of paper to inside of binder and glue. Cover binder with self-adhesive clear plastic film.

**3** Mount photos on paper using adhesive photo corners. Then slip the completed page inside a clear plastic pocket to protect it.

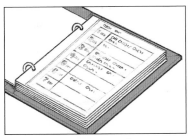

**4** Vaccination certificates, insurance papers, pedigrees, not to mention cat show awards, are also best protected inside clear plastic pockets.

# For Gourmet Cats

Cats have finely tuned taste buds, and some would rather starve than stoop to eating scraps. Discerning tabbies adore tasty morsels, attractively presented. Read on for a wealth of recipes sufficiently scrumptious for even the most refined pedigree's palette.

# Canapés for Cats

People parties can be excruciating for a gourmet cat. All those mouth-watering scents drifting from the kitchen are enough to drive your feline into a frenzy.

So why not make a special treat for your furry friend at the same time?

Remember, such savory treats are strictly for special occasions and should be served in moderation.

## Salmon Shapes

Place slices of smoked salmon onto thin slices of lightly buttered wholegrain bread. Cut into small fish shapes and serve.

## Chicken Nuggets

Wrap bite-sized pieces of chicken or turkey in thin slices of ham. Tie each bundle with a blade of grass picked from the garden or from your indoor grass tray (see page 46).

## Cream Confection

Alas, cats cannot taste sweet foods, so strawberries are wasted on them. But not so the cream! Most cats find whipped cream irresistible. Fill small pastry shells with cream. The shell may not be devoured, but the cream is sure to be lapped up instantly.

## Purr-fect Pinwheels

Spread strips of lightly grilled bacon with cream cheese. Roll them up and cut into pinwheels. Serve slightly chilled.

## Great Balls of Tuna

In a bowl, fold some cream or mayonnaise (whichever your cat prefers) into the contents of a small can of tuna. Form the mousse into lots of little tuna balls.

## Shrimp Surprise

If there's one food few cats can resist, it's shrimp. It's held in high esteem in most cat circles, and is almost as difficult to get hold of as caviar. Serve unadorned or garnish with a dollop of herb mayonnaise.

# Down-home Cooking

Rich foods such as cream and cheese are far from ideal for your cat's daily diet. But with little effort, you can make delicious home-cooked meals. Served as an alternative to good-quality, store-bought cat food, your home cooking will help to keep your cat in tip-top condition.

Cats enjoy primarily meat and fish. They can never be vegetarians, so don't be tempted to impose your garden creations on them.

Here are a few culinary basics that are sure to please cats and will provide lots of nutritional goodness.

## Chicken Casserole

Remove the skin from a piece of chicken and place the chicken in an ovenproof dish. Cover with cold water and add a few slivers of a chicken bouillon cube. Cover the dish and place in the microwave. Cook according to the manufacturer's recommended cooking times. When slightly cooled, take the chicken off the bone, and cut up the meat into bite-sized pieces. About 4 oz of cooked meat with a little stock provides the perfect evening meal for an adult cat.

**Variation:**
For a proven favorite, substitute rabbit for chicken.

## Basic Fish Dish

Place white fish, such as cod or haddock, in an ovenproof dish. Cover with half milk and half water and simmer until done. When slightly cooled, remove the skin and any bones, flake the fish, and serve. About 4 oz. of fish is ideal for an adult cat's breakfast or evening meal.

**Variation:**
Add a little smoked fish for added flavor.

## Scrambled Eggs

Lightly scramble an egg – no milk or salt, just an egg. When cooled, chop it and serve. It will prove popular, but only serve once a week. Slivers of grilled bacon can be added.

# Cat Place Mat

Even fastidious felines can spill their food, and lots of kitties even prefer eating from the floor. They'll take chunks of food from the dish to eat on the mat. So it makes sense to provide a washable place mat for food and water bowls.

You can easily make one from boldly colored oilcloth or plastic. Buy the heaviest weight you can find, then cut out a simple rectangle or a cat-friendly shape like a fish or mouse. You can do this by scaling up one of the motifs on pages 58–63.

Before you cut, be sure the mat is big enough. Better too big than too small when it comes to keeping your cat's dining space clean and tidy.

## Materials Needed
- Plastic fabric: 18 in. square
- Pencil and paper
- Scissors

45

# Green Gifts

Owners of outdoor cats know that cats like to nibble grass. It aids digestion and provides extra vitamins.

An indoor cat also needs to eat grass now and then. Grass-growing kits are available from pet stores and it's easy to grow small amounts of grass from seed in a covered plant propagator box or a shallow tray. Sow a new batch of grass every month so that your cat is never short of fresh greenery.

Catnip, also known as catmint (*Nepeta cataria*), is an herb belonging to the mint family. It contains oils that send lots of cats into delighted frenzies. It is easy to grow too. Keep a pot of it for special occasions – your cat will be ecstatic!

## Materials Needed
- Small seed tray or plant propagator with lid
- Flowerpots (optional)
- Planting soil
- Grass seed from pet store or top quality lawn seed or catnip seed

**1** Fill a seed tray with soil. Sprinkle a handful of your chosen seed over the surface. (If only top quality lawn seed is available, check with your local pet store or veterinarian that it contains nothing unsuitable for cat consumption). Lightly cover the seed with soil.

**2** Thoroughly moisten soil. Fit the lid on the propagator. Leave in a warm, dark place. Water as necessary to keep soil moist. When the seedlings appear, move the tray into the light and maintain watering.

**3** Cats love to find treats in unexpected places. So transplant the plants into smaller containers and put them in various locations around your home that your cat can get at. Remember to water plants regularly.

**4** Catnip is decorative, so put it in pretty pots. Either grow from seed, or buy plants from a garden center. Always keep some catnip in reserve – your cat may go wild with delight and dig up an entire pot in minutes.

# That's My Bowl

Your cat is likely to be highly possessive about eating equipment. Be sure that everyone knows which is the cat's bowl by marking it on the outside with its name, initials, or a special cat motif. Bowls made out of enameled metal, plastic, or ceramic can all be decorated in this way. Draw your own design freehand or use one of the templates.

### Materials Needed
- Food bowl
- Stencil board or acetate
- Washable felt-tip pen
- Craft knife
- Cutting mat
- Masking tape
- Flat paintbrush
- Ceramic tile or old plate
- Stencil brush
- Non-toxic enamel paints

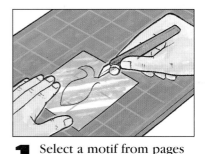

**1** Select a motif from pages 58–63. Reduce it to the correct size for your cat's bowl. Trace the shape onto stencil board or acetate. Use a craft knife to cut the stencil.

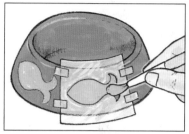

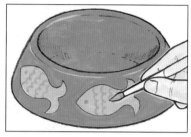

**2** Position the stencil on the bowl with masking tape. Apply a thin film of paint to the tile with the flat brush. Holding the stencil brush upright, dab into paint and through stencil.

**3** Let each motif dry completely before starting work on the next. Use the flat brush to add details in another color. Dry for several days before using the bowl.

# Purr-fect Presentation

Cats, like children, often find festive gift wrap
more intriguing than the present inside.
Crackling tissue paper and sparkling silk
ribbon will prove irresistible.

# Card and Wrap

Crisp, crunchy paper – half the fun of a gift is ripping off the wrapping. Cats will be eager to participate and will enjoy having their own packages to tear open.

Brightly colored tissue paper is ideal for wrapping cat gifts. Put it loosely round your present and hold it in place with wide, cloth ribbon. A pinch of catnip inside the wrappings will give most cats the incentive to get their claws into their gift.

For birthdays, a hand-made card shows your cat that you really care. Follow these simple instructions to make a card with cat appeal.

## Materials Needed

- Heavy paper: 5 in. square
- Pencil and ruler
- Craft knife
- Cutting mat
- Colored pencils or felt-tip pens

**1** Draw a faint horizontal rule through the center of the paper in pencil. Trace a cat's head motif (see page 61) onto the paper. The base of the ears should sit on the center line.

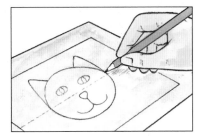

**2** Using a craft knife, carefully cut around ears and top of head so this section is separate. Bend the card along the center line so the ears stand up.

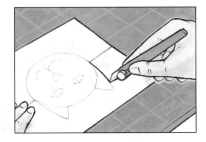

**3** Decorate the face using felt-tip pens or colored pencils. Add a bow under kitty's chin. If you have a black cat, use black paper and paint on white features. Don't forget the whiskers. Write your loving message inside.

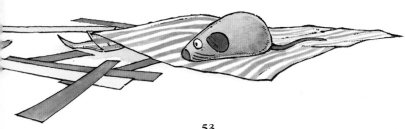

# Christmas Stocking

What Christmas could be complete without the joy of delving into trinket-filled stockings? Let kitty join in the excitement, too. This festive stocking will hold all your cat's favorite Christmas treats. It is made of felt and will withstand energetic burrowing year after year. The bells on the trim make great toys, but make sure they are really large so kitty can't swallow them! Items with a strong scent will entice curious and greedy cats to investigate. The gifts listed here have proved particularly successful with our team of four-pawed experts. A new catnip mouse (see page 13) will keep kitty happy most of the day. A handful of dried cat treats are always a hit, as is a painted ball (see page 9). And long silk ribbons will provide plenty of opportunities for play.

## Materials Needed

- Red felt: 36 in. square
- Green felt: 2 pieces, 10 in. x 3 in. each
- Black felt: 6 in. square for each cat motif
- Double-sided fusable interfacing: 6 in. square
- Plaid ribbon: ⅝ in. x 9 in. for each cat motif
- Embroidery thread in contrasting colors for cat's features
- Large bells: 6
- Basic sewing equipment

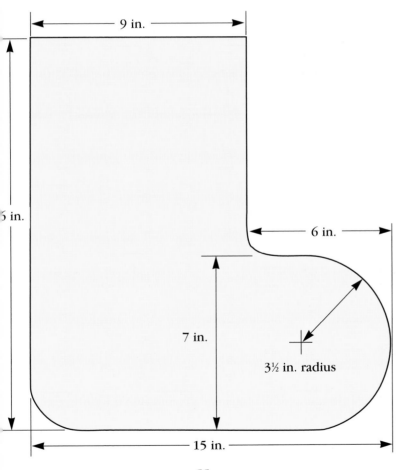

**1** Make a paper pattern (see previous page) and enlarge as desired. Fold the red felt in half. Pin the pattern to the double thickness of red felt. Cut through both layers to make two stocking shapes.

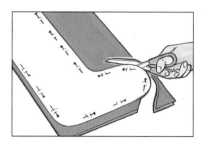

**2** Fuse interfacing to the black felt, following the manufacturer's instructions. Draw a cat outline, traced from the motif on page 63, onto the backing paper. Cut out one motif, or two if you prefer to have one on each side.

**3** Remove the backing paper and fuse the cat motif to the right side of one of the stocking pieces. Embroider eyes, nose, and whiskers in position, as marked on the template.

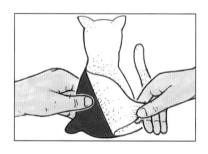

**4** Take the pieces of green felt and cut one long edge of each piece into three large points as shown. Stitch the straight edge of each piece to the top of each stocking piece. Press and baste to the stocking along the side edges.

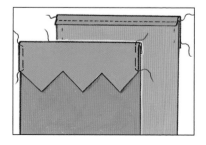

**5** Place stocking pieces together, right sides out. Machine stitch along raw edges, leaving top open.

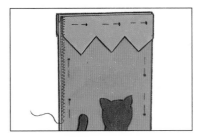

**6** Sew a large bell to each point of the green trim, *not* small enough for your cat to swallow. Stitch a bow to the cat motif.

# Motifs

The motifs on the following pages have been especially selected for their cat appeal. Check each project to see if you can use the template in the size shown, or if you need to make them bigger or smaller.

## Just the right size

If the motif size shown is right for your project, then photocopy or trace it. Cut out the photocopy to create the pattern, or transfer your tracing to thick cardboard or paper before cutting.

## Changing sizes

If you want to make your motif bigger or smaller, by far the easiest way is to use a photocopier which can enlarge or reduce the image. If you

don't have access to a photocopier, you will need to use the grid method to alter the size of the motif or pattern.

If you want to make the motifs much smaller, buy some grid paper with divisions as small as an ⅛ in. If you want to make them bigger, buy grid paper divided into 1 in. squares. The grid lines in this book are ½ in. apart.

On your grid paper, roughly sketch in pencil the motif at your chosen size. Now draw the motif much more carefully, copying across the outline square by square. Notice the points where the outline crosses the lines of the original grid. Make sure it crosses the corresponding lines of your own grid.

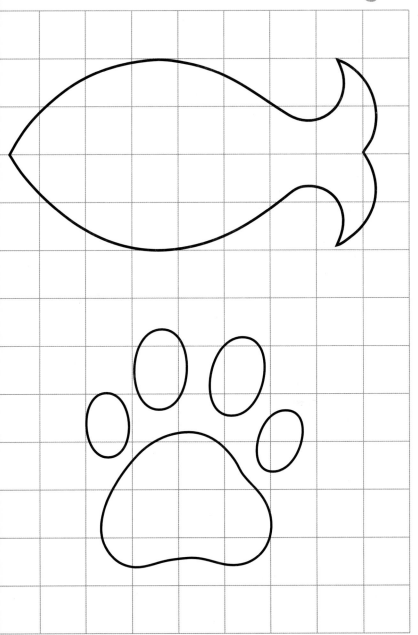

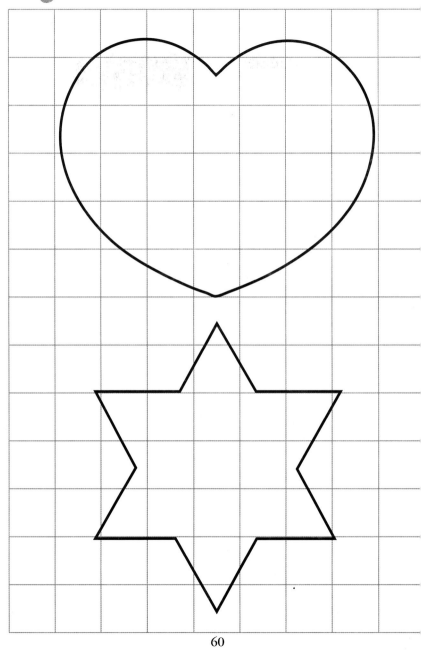

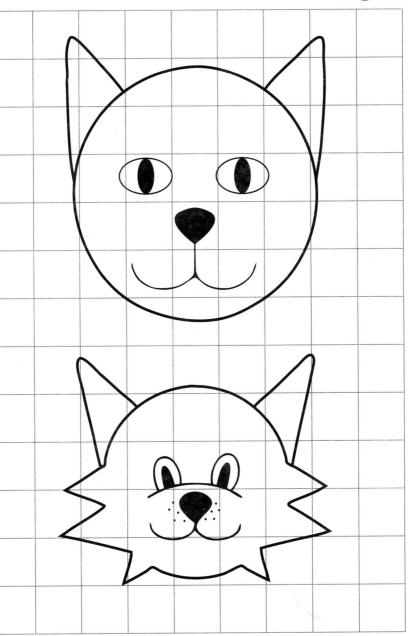

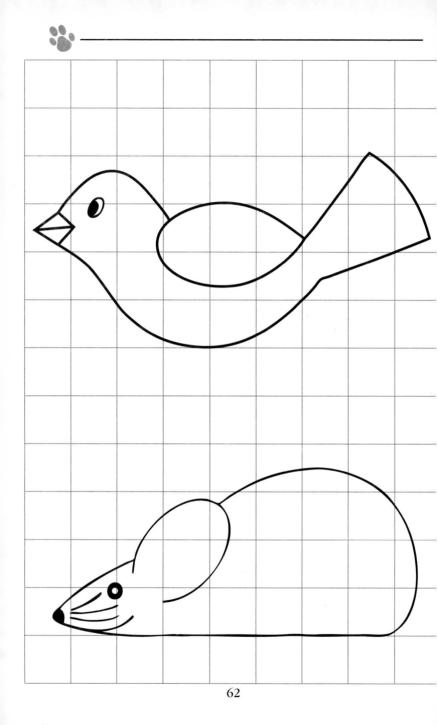

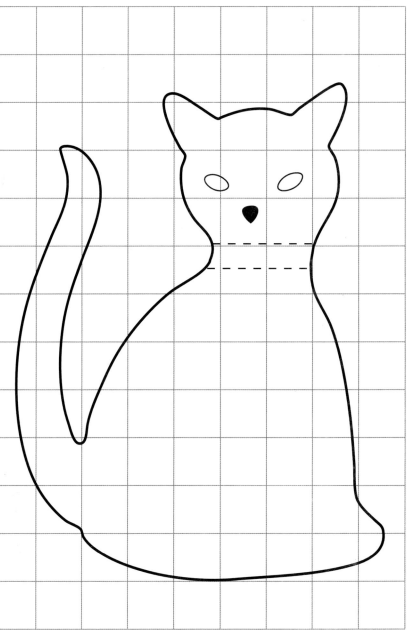

# Sewing Notes

All the items in this book have been designed to be quick and easy to make. And remember, most cats are not all that critical. A sewing machine is the easiest way to make the cloth gifts, but they can be made by hand. Use back stitch for hand-sewn seams. The other stitches are mentioned throughout the book and pictured here for easy reference.

Before you begin a sewing project, you should have the following basic equipment to hand.

BASIC SEWING EQUIPMENT
Scissors
Sewing thread
Needles and pins
Thimble (if you use one)
Ruler
Tape measure
Paper and pencil
Tracing paper

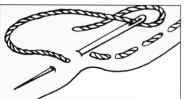

Back stitch

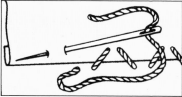

Slipstitch

Blanket stitch

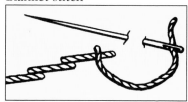

Stem stitch

Running stitch